New Mexico
Facts and Symbols

by Shelley Swanson Sateren

Consultant:
Sandra L. Gray, Ed.S.
New Mexico Council for the Social Studies
Albuquerque, New Mexico, Public Schools

Hilltop Books
an imprint of Capstone Press
Mankato, Minnesota

Hilltop Books are published by Capstone Press
818 North Willow Street, Mankato, Minnesota 56001
http://www.capstone-press.com

Printed in the United States of America.

Library of Congress Cataloging-in-Publication Data
Sateren, Shelley Swanson.
New Mexico facts and symbols / by Shelley Swanson Sateren.
p. cm.—(The states and their symbols)
Includes bibliographical references and index.
Summary: Presents information about the state of New Mexico, its nickname, flag, motto, and emblems.
ISBN 0-7368-0380-7
1. Emblems, State—New Mexico—Juvenile literature. [1. Emblems, State—New Mexico. 2. New Mexico.] I. Title. II. Series.
CR203.N69S27 2000
978.9—dc21

99-31829
CIP

Editorial Credits
Christy Steele, editor; Heather Kindseth, cover designer; Linda Clavel, illustrator; Kimberly Danger, photo researcher

Photo Credits
Index Stock, cover
International Stock/Tom Till, 22 (top)
John Elk III, 16
Kent and Donna Dannen, 6
One Mile Up, Inc., 8, 10 (inset)
Photophile/Roger Holden, 22 (bottom)
Root Resources/Ruth A. Smith, 14; Bill Glass, 22 (middle)
Visuals Unlimited/Link, 10; Maslowski, 12; Erwin C. "Bud" Nielsen, 18; Rob and Ann Simpson, 20

The author wishes to thank Robert J. Torrez for his assistance in preparing this book.

Table of Contents

Utah
Colorado
Oklahoma
Sangre De Cristo Mountains
Santa Fe
Petroglyph National Monument
Albuquerque
Acoma Pueblo
Arizona
NEW MEXICO
Texas
Rio Grande River
Lincoln National Forest
Carlsbad Caverns National Park
Mexico
Capital
City
Forest
Mountains
Places to Visit
River

Fast Facts

Capital City: Santa Fe is New Mexico's capital.
Largest City: New Mexico's largest city is Albuquerque. About 419,700 people live in this city.
Size: New Mexico covers 121,598 square miles (314,939 square kilometers). It is the fifth largest state.
Location: New Mexico is in the southwestern United States.
Population: 1,736,931 people live in New Mexico (U.S. Census Bureau, 1998 estimate).
Statehood: New Mexico became the 47th state on January 6, 1912.
Natural Resources: New Mexican miners dig up copper. Workers mine sand and gravel for use in construction projects.
Manufactured Goods: New Mexican workers make electronics, machines, food products, and clothing.
Crops: New Mexican farmers grow pecans, onions, chiles, and cotton. They also grow grasses to make hay. Livestock farmers raise cattle, hogs, and sheep.

State Name and Nickname

About 500 years ago, Spanish explorers claimed the land that is now New Mexico for Spain. They called the land Nuevo Mejico (noo-AYE-voh MEH-hee-koh). This name means New Mexico in Spanish.

New Mexico does not have an official state nickname. About 100 years ago, people began to call New Mexico the Land of Sunshine. New Mexico became known for its sunny weather. Government and tourism workers began using the nickname to draw visitors to the state.

In 1906, a book published about New Mexico called it the Land of Enchantment. The author believed the state's deserts and mountains charmed people as if by magic. This phrase became New Mexico's most popular nickname. In 1941, officials put this nickname on New Mexico license plates. Today, the New Mexico Department of Tourism uses this phrase.

People nicknamed New Mexico the Land of Sunshine because of its sunny weather.

GREAT SEAL OF THE STATE OF NEW MEXICO
1912
Crescit Eundo

State Seal and Motto

New Mexico adopted its state seal in 1913. The seal reminds New Mexicans of their state government. The seal also makes government papers official.

Two eagles are on New Mexico's state seal. The large bald eagle stands for the United States. One of the eagle's wings shields a smaller Mexican eagle. This picture represents the New Mexico Territory becoming part of the United States in 1846.

The Mexican eagle carries a snake in its beak. The eagle's claws grip a cactus. This picture stands for an ancient Aztec story. The Aztecs are a native people of New Mexico.

New Mexico's motto is "Crescit Eundo" (KRES-kit eh-OON-doh). This Latin phrase means "it grows as it goes." Crescit Eundo stands for New Mexicans' belief in growth and progress.

The year 1912 appears at the bottom of New Mexico's state seal. New Mexico became a state during this year.

SEAL OF THE STATE OF NEW
1912

State Capitol and Flag

New Mexico's capitol building is in Santa Fe. Santa Fe is the capital of New Mexico. Government officials meet in the capitol to make state laws.

New Mexico's first capitol was the Palace of the Governors. Spain built the capitol when it ruled New Mexico. Later, officials from Mexico and the United States worked in the building. Today, the Palace of the Governors is a museum.

New Mexico workers finished building the current capitol in 1966. The building is the only round capitol in the United States. The building is shaped like a Zia sun symbol. The Zia is a circle with 16 rays. This symbol is a Pueblo Indian sign of perfection. The Pueblo were among New Mexico's first settlers.

The New Mexican government adopted its state flag in 1925. The flag is yellow with a red Zia symbol in the center.

The Zia's rays stand for the four directions, the four parts of a day, the four stages of life, and the four seasons of the year.

State Bird

In 1932, New Mexicans voted the roadrunner their favorite bird. Officials made the roadrunner New Mexico's state bird in 1949. People often see roadrunners running along New Mexican highways.

Roadrunners are long birds. Adults are 20 inches (51 centimeters) long. Their tails are as long as their bodies. Roadrunners also have long bills.

Brown feathers with white streaks cover roadrunners' bodies. The birds have bushy feather crests on their heads. In sunlight, the feathers look olive green. This color helps camouflage the birds from predators. Olive green blends well with cactus plants that grow in New Mexico's deserts.

Roadrunners can fly. But they usually run. Roadrunners can run up to 20 miles (32 kilometers) per hour. Pioneers nicknamed the birds roadrunners. They saw the birds running in the ruts made by wagon wheels.

Roadrunners eat lizards, scorpions, tarantulas, snakes, and mice.

State Tree

New Mexico officials asked the New Mexico Federation of Women's Clubs to choose a state tree. The women chose the piñon. Piñon forests cover more than one-quarter of New Mexico. Officials agreed with the women's choice. They made the piñon the state tree in 1949.

The piñon is a member of the pine family. The tree has dark green needles. Piñons grow slowly. The trees grow only 20 to 40 feet (6 to 12 meters) tall.

Piñons have egg-shaped cones that hold seeds. Each fall, the cones open. Tiny piñon seeds drop to the ground. People gather, roast, and eat the seeds. New Mexicans call the seeds piñon nuts. Some companies prepare and sell piñon nuts.

Lumber companies once sold much piñon wood for firewood. Today, New Mexico is limiting the sale of piñon wood to save piñon trees.

Piñon trees grow well in dry, rocky soil.

State Flower

The yucca (YUH-ka) is New Mexico's state flower. New Mexican schoolchildren chose the yucca as the state flower. The government made the children's choice official in 1927. Many yucca plants grow on New Mexico's deserts and plains.

Stiff, pointed leaves grow from the yucca's base. The leaves look like green spikes. Yucca leaves grow up to 2 feet (.6 meters) long. Native Americans once used the leaves' tips as needles. They used the leaves' bases as paintbrushes.

One tall, thin stalk grows from the center of the yucca plant. About 20 to 60 waxy flowers grow on the stalk. Each flower has three white petals. Yucca flowers bloom in early summer.

Long ago, Native Americans found many uses for yucca flowers. They ate the flowers in salads. They ground yucca roots and used the powder to make soap and shampoo.

Yucca flowers grow well in the white sand of New Mexico's deserts.

State Animal

Officials named the black bear New Mexico's state animal in 1963. Many black bears live in the mountains and forests of New Mexico.

New Mexicans chose the black bear to honor Smokey Bear. In 1950, Smokey Bear was rescued from a forest fire in New Mexico. He survived by holding onto a burning tree. The U.S. Forest Service used Smokey Bear to teach people about forest fires.

Smokey Bear died in 1976. He is buried in a park named for him. People can visit his grave at Smokey Bear State Park in New Mexico.

Black bears are not always black. They can be brown or red-brown. Some black bears appear slightly blue or orange. A rare kind of black bear is white. White black bears also are called spirit bears.

Black bears eat piñon nuts, acorns, and berries. They turn over rocks to find grubs and other insects. They also eat animals such as rabbits.

Black bears are medium-sized bears. Adults weigh 200 to 600 pounds (91 to 272 kilograms).

More State Symbols

State Cookie: Officials chose biscochito (biss-ko-CHEE-toh) to be New Mexico's state cookie in 1989. Anise (AN-iss) seeds give these small sugar cookies a licorice flavor.

State Vegetables: Officials made the pinto bean and the chile pepper New Mexico's state vegetables in 1965. Pinto beans and chile peppers flavor many southwestern dishes.

State Fish: The New Mexico cutthroat trout became the state fish in 1955. This fish has red streaks under its throat. The cutthroat is native to northern New Mexico's cold mountain lakes.

State Insect: Officials made the tarantula hawk wasp the state insect in 1989. These New Mexican insects hunt tarantulas. Young wasps eat the tarantulas.

State Question: In 1996, officials chose "Red or Green?" to be the state question. Waiters in New Mexican restaurants ask this question to find out if people want red or green chiles on their food.

A tarantula hawk wasp's sting makes tarantulas unable to move.

Places to Visit

Acoma Pueblo

Acoma Pueblo is an ancient Native American village west of Albuquerque. The village sits on a mesa high above the desert. A mesa is a hill with steep sides and a flat top. People often call the village Sky City because of its location. Visitors walk through Acoma Pueblo and tour a museum.

Carlsbad Caverns National Park

Carlsbad Caverns National Park lies in southeastern New Mexico. The park has the world's largest natural underground chamber and more than 80 limestone caves. Visitors walk through these giant caves to see rock and mineral growths. Thousands of Mexican free-tailed bats live there.

Petroglyph National Monument

Petroglyph National Monument is near Albuquerque. Native Americans and Spanish explorers often camped by these extinct volcanoes. During the past 12,000 years, people carved pictures into the rocks. Today, visitors see more than 17,000 of these ancient petroglyphs.

Words to Know

anise (AN-iss)—a plant that has seeds used in medicine and cooking; anise seeds have a licorice flavor.
enchantment (en-CHANT-muhnt)—to feel charmed or under the spell of magic
mesa (MAY-suh)—a hill with steep sides and a flat top; mesas are common in southwestern deserts.
petroglyph (PEH-trah-glif)—a drawing or carving on rock usually made by ancient people
stalk (STALK)—a stem of a plant; the stalk supports or connects parts of a plant.

Read More

Fradin, Judith Bloom and Dennis B. Fradin. *New Mexico.* From Sea to Shining Sea. Chicago: Children's Press, 1993.
Kent, Deborah. *New Mexico.* America the Beautiful. New York: Children's Press, 1999.
Kummer, Patricia K. *New Mexico.* One Nation. Mankato, Minn.: Capstone Press, 1998.
McDaniel, Melissa. *New Mexico.* Celebrate the States. New York: Benchmark Books, 1999.

Useful Addresses

New Mexico Department of Tourism
491 Old Santa Fe Trail
P.O. Box 20002
Santa Fe, NM 87501

New Mexico Secretary of State
State Capitol, Room 420
Santa Fe, NM 87503

Internet Sites

New Mexico Department of Tourism—Land of Enchantment
http://www.newmexico.org

Viva New Mexico
http://www.vivanewmexico.com

Welcome to New Mexico!
http://www.state.nm.us

Index